Pisa
Travel Guide

Quick Trips Series

No part of this publication may be reproduced, stored in a retrieval system, or transmitted, in any form or by any means without the prior written permission of the publisher, nor be otherwise circulated in any form of binding or cover other than that in which it is published and without similar condition being imposed on the subsequent purchaser. If there are any errors or omissions in copyright acknowledgements the publisher will be pleased to insert the appropriate acknowledgement in any subsequent printing of this publication. Although we have taken all reasonable care in researching this book we make no warranty about the accuracy or completeness of its content and disclaim all liability arising from its use.

Copyright © 2016, Astute Press
All Rights Reserved.

Table of Contents

PISA — 7
- 🌐 CUSTOMS & CULTURE 10
- 🌐 GEOGRAPHY 11
- 🌐 WEATHER & BEST TIME TO VISIT 11

SIGHTS & ACTIVITIES: WHAT TO SEE & DO — 14
- 🌐 PIAZZA DEI MIRACOLI (SQUARE OF MIRACLES) 14
- 🌐 LEANING TOWER OF PISA 16
- 🌐 BELL TOWER OF SAN NICOLA CHURCH 23
- 🌐 DUOMO DI PISA (CATHEDRAL OF PISA) 24
- 🌐 BATTISTERO (BAPTISTERY) 27
- 🌐 CAMPOSANTO (WALLED CEMETERY) 31
- 🌐 MUSEO DELL'OPERA DEL DUOMO 33
- 🌐 MUSEO NAZIONALE DI SAN MATTEO 36
- 🌐 PALAZZO DELL' OROLOGIO 38
- 🌐 CAMPANILE DI SAN NICOLA (ST. NICOLAS BELFRY) 40
- 🌐 MUSEUM OF THE ANCIENT SHIPS 41
- 🌐 USSERO CAFÉ 43

BUDGET TIPS — 46
- 🌐 ACCOMMODATION 46

- Hotel Granduca Tuscany 46
- Hotel Capitol 47
- Hotel la Torre 48
- Hotel Francesco 49
- Eden Park Tuscany Resort 50

◉ Restaurants, Cafés & Bars 51
- Il Montino 51
- Ristorante Turrido 51
- Peperosa Pisa 52
- L'Ostellino 53
- Coccio Bar & Gelateria 53

◉ Shopping 54
- Corso Italia 54
- Borgo Stretto 55
- Piazza dei Cavalieri & Ponti di Mezzo 56
- Piazza delle Vettovaglie 56
- Via Buonarroti & Via San Martino 57

KNOW BEFORE YOU GO   59

◉ Entry Requirements 59
◉ Health Insurance 59
◉ Travelling with Pets 60
◉ Airports 60
◉ Airlines 62
◉ Currency 63
◉ Banking & ATMs 63
◉ Credit Cards 63
◉ Tourist Taxes 64
◉ Reclaiming VAT 64
◉ Tipping Policy 65
◉ Mobile Phones 65

- Dialling Code 66
- Emergency Numbers 66
- Public Holidays 67
- Time Zone 68
- Daylight Savings Time 68
- School Holidays 68
- Trading Hours 69
- Driving Laws 69
- Drinking Laws 70
- Smoking Laws 71
- Electricity 71
- Tourist Information (TI) 72
- Food & Drink 72
- Websites 74

PISA TRAVEL GUIDE

PISA TRAVEL GUIDE

Pisa

Pisa is a famous city in Italy that is best known for the world famous Leaning Tower but which offers much more. Pisa offers some of the most beautiful views of the Tuscan mountains and is just a short drive away from the scenic hill towns and villages of Tuscany.

Pisa was a bustling port in the 10th and 11th centuries. In 1944 during the Second World War, Pisa was attacked for 45 days. Thousands of its inhabitants were killed and half of the city's buildings were destroyed. Despite this the architecture, art and sculpture of the city are still its biggest attractions.

Pisa has retained so much of its historical look and feel that UNESCO has named it a World Heritage site.

PISA TRAVEL GUIDE

Because the city center is quite small the best way to enjoy the sights is to walk the streets of the old city. Some of the most famous examples of architectural treasures in Pisa can be found in the Piazza deiMiracoli or Square of Miracles. This is a very large square with an immaculately tended lawn that has been there since the 11th century and which lies next to medieval walls that are still standing in the heart of the old city. The four marble buildings that rise out of that lawn combine the architecture of the Moors along with Celtic and Roman architecture and are some of Italy's most famous landmarks. The buildings include the cathedral known as the Duomo di Pisa, the world famous Leaning Tower of Pisa which was built as a bell tower for the cathedral, the

PISA TRAVEL GUIDE

Baptistery and the Monumental churchyard or Camposanto.

Throngs of travelers come to see these architectural marvels every year making Pisa one of the most important tourist sites in Italy. But that is not all that Pisa has to offer. The city also boasts several museums which are worth visiting for the architecture of the buildings themselves as well as the art and sculpture on display inside. Pisa's museums contain the works of many of the great Italian artists and are a must see for anyone with an appreciation of beauty and form.

The great physicist and astronomer Galileo Galilei was born in Pisa and his birthplace is still clearly marked and the city's international airport is named after him. Galileo

PISA TRAVEL GUIDE

attended the university in Pisa and studied for a medical degree before becoming a scientist. According to local folklore Galileo is said to have dropped objects from the tower of Pisa in an effort to see if heavier objects fell faster than smaller ones of the same material. There is no evidence to prove that this really happened but it is a great story to tell just the same.

Like pretty much anywhere else in Italy the food in Pisa is a gourmand's delight. Because it lies on the coast, Pisa is well known for its seafood dishes such as 'Bavettine Sui Pesce' which is flattened spaghetti seasoned with a delicious white sauce, mussels soup which is served on Tuscan bread and Frog soup. If seafood is not your favorite, however, the city also offers delectable land dishes and of course desserts, a favorite of which is the

PISA TRAVEL GUIDE

'tortacoivischeri' which is a cake made with pine-seeds, raisins, chocolate and citrus candy. There is also a variety of local wines to accompany all the wonderful food.

Customs & Culture

Pisa is a university town with the University of Pisa students numbering 60,000 in a city that only 100,000 people call home. The university is one of Italy's oldest. It was established in 1343 and is considered one of country's best. Pisa is also home to the Scuola Normale Superiore an educational institute which has its origins in Paris and which has been around since 1810. Only the best students were admitted to this institute and it is still considered an elite school.

PISA TRAVEL GUIDE

The city of Pisa has the vibe that all university towns have where you feel that a party can get started anywhere at any time and the students do often organize parties and other music events that are open to the public. There are of course nightclubs in Pisa as well as several pubs and pizza parlors such as the Millie Bar that boasts a vibrant Karaoke night every Tuesday because everyone knows that Italians love to sing. Many visitors enjoy just walking around the city center at night alongside the low walls around the river. Because it is a university city there are also always low priced accommodations available for the budget traveler.

🌍 Geography

Pisa is a city in the region of Tuscany, in Central Italy in the province of Pisa, close to Lucca and Florence. It is

PISA TRAVEL GUIDE

one of the chief towns in that region. It is located on the bank of the mouth of the River Arno on the Tyrrhenian Sea.

🌍 Weather & Best Time to Visit

Pisa has warm, sunny summers as is common in the Mediterranean with the peak summer months of June to August being quiet hot and Pisa experiences temperatures of 30 degrees Centigrade regularly. In the wintertime it is cooler and quite wet and fog is a possibility. Although it doesn't really get very cold it can get windy so warm clothes are needed if you are going to visit between November and February.

If you are lucky enough to be in Pisa on the 16th of June you will witness the Luminara festival or Fiesta di san

PISA TRAVEL GUIDE

Ranieri. This festival is held to celebrate the city's patron saints day. In the evening of that day all the lights along the river go out or are lowered and 10,000 candles or torches are lit. There are also street events and fireworks displays. The city's monuments look even more beautiful by candlelight and this festival should not be missed.

One of the city's largest events is the Giocodel Ponte or Game of the Bridge which also takes place in the month of June and which has been around since the 16th century. The Game involves a series of challenges among twelve teams made up of people from the north and south banks of the city. They dress in medieval costumes.

PISA TRAVEL GUIDE

Sights & Activities: What to See & Do

🌍 Piazza dei Miracoli (Square of Miracles)

56010 Pisa, Italy

The Piazza del Miracoli or Square of Miracles is a walled square located in central Pisa which dates back to the pre-Roman era. It is famous for the architecture of the

PISA TRAVEL GUIDE

building that can be found there as well as its cultural heritage and has been named by UNESCO as a World Heritage Site. It was given its name by the Italian poet Gabriele D'Annunzio who described the square that way in one of his books and is not to be confused with the Campo deiMiracoli in the fictional story of Pinnocchio.

The large square is also sometimes called the Piazza del Duomo after one of the buildings there. Made mostly of grass but with some paved areas, the Piazza is best known for the 4 marble buildings which stand in it and which are some of the most famous buildings in the world. All built between the 11th and 14th century, the four religious structures are the Duomo or Cathedral, the Campanile or bell tower, the Battistero or Baptistery and the Composanto or walled cemetery.

PISA TRAVEL GUIDE

Apart from the four famous structures the square is also home to the OspedaleNuovo di Santo Spirito which was built as a hospital in the 13th century by Italian architect Giovanni di Simone. Its name translates to the new Hospital of the Holy Spirit but it is now home to the museum of Sinopias which you can visit to view the original drawings of the walled cemetery which is also located in the field. The hospital is made of red brick unlike the other buildings in the square which are white marble and it was restructured in 1562.

The Square of Miracles is considered to be one of the best places in the world for viewing and appreciating medieval art. Everyone who visits Pisa spends some time

PISA TRAVEL GUIDE

there and it is very easy to reach from either the airport or the train station.

🌍 Leaning Tower of Pisa

Piazza Arcivescovado, 6, Pisa

The Leaning Tower of Pisa is also called Le Torre Pisa or la Campanile (a bell tower that is free-standing).

It was built as the bell tower of the city's cathedral and the objective was to demonstrate the wealth of the city at the time. It is now considered one of the seven wonders of the Medieval World. When work began on the Tower in August of 1173, its design and the way it was being constructed was ahead of its time.

PISA TRAVEL GUIDE

The intention was that the Tower would be vertical but after the 3rd floor was built it began to lean. The reason was not known at the time but it has since been discovered that the Tower was built on a clay mixture which was too soft to support the construction without sinking and the foundation was only 3 meters deep so the building began to lean in a southwesterly direction. Despite this, or perhaps because of it, the tower is considered the world over to be a great work of art and many people visit Pisa just to see it.

When the lean was first noticed in 1178, work on the Tower stopped. It began again in 1272 under the direction of Giovanni did Simone but stopped again in 1284 because of the battle of Meloria against the people of

PISA TRAVEL GUIDE

Genoa, Pisa's enemies at that time. The Pisans lost that battle.

The design of the Tower would be worth seeing even if it did not lean. The exterior is made of white marble and under the marble is limestone and lime mortar and it is that material that is most likely responsible for the fact that the building is still standing. The tower of Pisa rises 55 meters into the air and has 8 stories. The stories are made up of marble columns stacked on top of each other. There are over 200 Corinthian columns in all. The floors at the top of the tower were built out from the vertical in the direction opposite to where the tower leans in an effort to serve as a counter balance.

PISA TRAVEL GUIDE

On the bottom story of the tower there are 15 marble arches. The tower weighs over 14 hundred tons, has 207 columns, 30 arches on each level above the ground floor and is said to be listing by about 10%. The inside walls of the cylindrical tower as well as the outer walls are made of limestone and it is hollow inside. There's a spiral staircase that is also made of marble and which is made up of 294 steps. The stairway goes up to the sixth level and in the actual bell chamber there are seven bells which are all properly tuned. The bells are housed in cells like windows. The bell chamber was completed in 1372 and work on the tower stopped after that until the 1800s.

When the bell tower was built 7 bells were put in. Each bell had a name. They were called L'Assunta, Il Crocifisso, San Ranieri, La Pasquereccia, Del Pozzetto,

PISA TRAVEL GUIDE

La Terza and Il Vespruccio. La Pasquereccia is the oldest bell. It was cast in 1262 by Lotteringo and carries an inscription that indicates when it was made and by whom. It also says that the bell was paid for by someone called Gerardo Hospilatarius.

The engravings on the bell include drawings of animals, angels and other religious depictions. Before it was put in the Tower the Pasquereccia was the bell used in the Tower of Justice to announce when criminals were being executed. It was most likely rung when Count Ugolino died. The bell weighs over 2000 lbs. and is also called La Giustiza. The largest bell is L'Assunta, named after Our Lady of the Assumption, which is made of gold and was cast in 1654 by Giovanni Pietro. It weighs nearly 8,000 lbs and carries an inscription that says "The angels raise the

PISA TRAVEL GUIDE

Virgin Mary to heaven and rejoicing and praising, they bless Our Lord."

The bells were rung using a bell cord from the ground but there was concerned that the swinging could affect the Tower so that was stopped. It was replaced by clappers within the bells that are activated by electromagnets.

Several people have worked on the tower but no one knows architect designed it. It was finished by Tommaso Pisano who built the belfry. In 1838 an architect named Alessandro Della Gherardesca decided to put in a pathway at the base of the Tower so that visitors could see the intricate work done on the base of the Tower. This made the building lean more.

PISA TRAVEL GUIDE

In 1964 the Italian government led by Benito Mussolini, embarrassed by the continued leaning of the building asked for help and a team of professionals came together and decided to put in an 800 ton counter weight. They did this by drilling into the foundation and pouring in cement. Unfortunately the cement sank into the clay soil under the square and made things worse. The tower was closed to the public in 1990 in case the crowds make the leaning worse and it remained closed to visitors until 2001. The bells were removed and the building was anchored during that time. The engineers who worked on the Tower at that time believe that the building will remain at the angle it was then for several hundred years unless there is a major earthquake. It is currently open and a very popular site.

PISA TRAVEL GUIDE

If you plan to visit the Tower it is a good idea to book your ticket online or in person a couple of weeks in advance so that you can avoid the long lines and that way you can also ensure that the tickets don't sell out before you get yours. People who book in advance also go straight to the top of the line. Advance tickets to climb the tower cost 17 Euros which is 2 Euros more than if you buy your ticket at the box office but you will definitely be able to climb the tower that day.

Twice every hour people are allowed in and if you buy an advanced ticket you will be allocated a certain time to enter. You have to ensure that you are there at the time. It takes about 10 minutes to climb the stairs and many people have reported feeling dizzy because of the tilt of the building. The Tower is opened from 10 in the morning

PISA TRAVEL GUIDE

to 5 in the afternoon from November to February except for Christmas day and January 7 when the tower opens from 9 am to 6pm. From March 21 to June 15 the hours are 8:30 am to 8:30 pm. For the rest of June and until August 31 the tower is open to the public from 8:30 am to 11 pm. All through September you can visit the Tower from 8:30 am to 8:30 pm while the schedule for October is 9:00 am to 7:00 pm.

Bell Tower of San Nicola Church

Via Santa Maria

56100, Pisa, Italy

Known by locals as Campanile di San Nicola, the bell tower at San Nicola church is sometimes overlooked because of the popularity of the city's other bell tower, the

PISA TRAVEL GUIDE

Leaning Tower of Pisa, but it is certainly worth seeing. Built in the Pisan-Romanesque style of architecture, the eight-sided tower is also found in central Pisa and is actually also leaning a bit. The base is already below the level of the road.

No one is quite sure when the tower was built but researchers believe it was built in 1170 and that Diotisalvi was the architect. Different types of stones, such as limestone, Elba granite and Apuan marble were brought in from different locations to give the tower its multicolored look. The marble was used to construct the columns.

Inside the tower is a spiral staircase which researchers recently discovered was designed based on the geometric studies done by Pisan mathematician Leonardo

Fibonacci. The stairway has a wall on the external side only. The tower also has a roof that is shaped like a pyramid.

The bell-chamber of the tower has six sides and each side has a window. There is only one bell in the chamber. At present the public is not allowed inside the tower but the outside alone is worth the visit.

🌐 Duomo di Pisa (Cathedral of Pisa)

Piazza dei Miracoli

56010 Pisa, Italy

The Cathedral was the first building that was erected in the Square of Miracles. Construction began in 1064. The Catholic Cathedral is an example of Romanesque

PISA TRAVEL GUIDE

architecture although there are traces of other styles to be found on the building including the influence of the Arabs with whom Pisa had many battles. It was the spoils of some of these battles that were used to finance the construction of the cathedral. The Cathedral is one of the largest in the world and is nearly 600 years old. It is 30 stories high and has 464 steps which the public is allowed to climb. The outside walls are much more ornate than the inside.

The main architect of the structure was Buschelo and he is buried in the Cathedral. After him in the 12th century came the architect Rainaldo who built the white marble façade of the Cathedral. The stones on the exterior of the structure are engraved with ancient inscriptions. The Cathedral is sometimes referred to as the Primatial

PISA TRAVEL GUIDE

because the Archbishop of Pisa has been a primate since the year 1672.

In 1595 there was a fire in the cathedral that destroyed most of the medieval art that was displayed there. Luckily they were replaced by equally if not more beautiful works from the Renaissance era. Some of the original works survived the fire so there are also some medieval pieces such as the bronze door called the door of San Ranieri which was made in 1180 by Bonnano Pisano and which features scenes from the bible. The tomb of Emperor Henry VII which was done by Tino di Camaino in 1315 can be found in the cathedral as well as the bones of Pisa's patron saint Saint Ranieri. The Cathedral was consecrated in 1118 by Pope Gelasius II. Pope Gregory

PISA TRAVEL GUIDE

VIII was also buried in the cathedral but the tomb was destroyed by the fire of 1595.

There are many other works of art inside the Cathedral that are worth seeing such as an ornate pulpit by the Italian sculptor and painter Giovanni Pisano that depicts biblical scenes which is one of the Cathedral's biggest attractions and a crucifix by the sculptor Giambologna. The inside walls are made of black and white marble and there is a dome adorned with frescoes and a ceiling of gold which carries the coat of arms of the house of Medici. There is also a mosaic fresco on the wall above the main altar done by the great Florentine painter Cimabue with the help of his students. The Cathedral is also slightly tiled although unlike the Bell Tower it is hardly noticeable. All these pieces and more combine to make the cathedral or Duomo one of the premier edifices to visit in Tuscany.

🌐 Battistero (Baptistery)

Piazza dei Miracoli, 56126 Pisa, Italy

The official name of this structure which is also found in the square of Miracles is the St. John Baptistery and it is where baptisms were performed. The structure is the largest baptistery in Italy and is dedicated to St. John the Baptist. The Baptistery is taller than the leaning Tower of Pisa if the statue of John the Baptist at the top is included. The design is Roman but there is also evidence of Islamic influences and this is because construction on the

PISA TRAVEL GUIDE

baptistery started soon after the crusades. The Baptistery is made of marble.

•

Work began on this structure, which is nearly as big as the cathedral, in the year 1152 and was led by Diotisalvi. We know this because his name is carved on one of the interior pillars. Work stopped sometime after and a hundred years passed before work was again started on the baptistery because of a lack of funds. Construction was continued by Giovanni and Nicola Pisano and it was never finished until 1363. Because it took so long to complete, the baptistery has a mix of architectural styles with the lower portion being Romanesque and the upper section Gothic. The upper part of the building has the pointed arches associated with Gothic architecture while the lower portion has rounded gothic arches.

PISA TRAVEL GUIDE

There are even two domes with roofs that are half lead, half tiles. The Baptistery is a circular building several floors high with a carved marble exterior and columns right around. Diotisalvi did not have that shape in mind when he began construction but when he died his successor Nicola Pisano changed the plans to a more Gothic style and it is he who added an external roof over the internal pyramid roof. The shape was supposed to resemble that of the Holy Sepulcher. Inside the Baptistery there are 8 tall columns and 4 pillars which form the central area. The roof is made up of a double dome which has a very unusual shape and which was added at the end of construction in the 14th century. The outer walls are very ornate while the interior has little decoration.

PISA TRAVEL GUIDE

One of the main attractions of the Baptistery is a pulpit which the sculptor Nicola Pisano carved which can be found in the central area of the structure. The pulpit has six sides and on it there are scenes from the bible and other scenes such as one of a naked Hercules. It was created between 1255 and 1260. On one corner of the sculptor there is a carving of Daniel that supports that side. There is also an eight sided baptismal font which was created by Guido Bigarellie da Como in 1246. It is next to the pulpit which is another big attraction along with a bronze sculpture by ItaloGriselli.

The artwork on the walls of the Baptistery depicts the life of john the Baptist and on the upper floors there is a depiction of Jesus Christ flanked by John the Baptist and the Virgin Mary with angels all around. A spiral staircase which takes you up the women's gallery and another staircase takes you right into the dome.

The acoustics of the building is one of the most fascinating aspects of the Battistero. It came about because of the double roof and every half hour or so a choir sings so that the sound can be appreciated. If you can sing feel free to try it out. Like most of the buildings in the Square of Miracles the baptistery leans slightly.

🌍 Camposanto (Walled Cemetery)

Piazza dei Miracoli, 56126 Pisa

Founded in 1277 the cemetery was intended as a place for the stone and marble tombs called sarcophagi in which local aristocrats were buried and that were

PISA TRAVEL GUIDE

scattered all over the nearby cathedral. It was completed in 1464.the legend states that the soil of the cemetery was brought to Pisa at the end of the Crusades by Ubaldo de Lanfranch. It is thought to be holy soil taken from Golgotha, the place where Jesus Christ was crucified.

The cemetery has 43 arches and 2 magnificent bronze doors by Ghiberti which are some of the main attractions. One doorway has a Gothic Tabernacle which depicts the Virgin Mary with child and 4 saints. The doorways that you would see if you visited the baptistery are replicas as the originals are in the Museo dell'Opera del Duomo in order to conserve them. The building also contains many statues and carvings of gothic design and sculptures

PISA TRAVEL GUIDE

In the 14th century beautiful frescos were added to the inside of the walls. They were on the then controversial themes of Life and Death and were created by two artists who were very popular at the time, Francesco Traini and Bonamico Buffalmacco. These were later added to by other Italian artists who added stories of the saints and the Old Testament.

In the 16th century the tombs of members of the ruling Medici family and esteemed local university lecturers were also placed in the cemetery. It was later utilized as a museum.

During World War II, the Camposanto was badly damaged by a bomb dropped by the Allied forces in 1944. The bomb destroyed many priceless artifacts and efforts have been made to restore the building to its former glory and they have largely been successful.

🌎 Museo dell'Opera del Duomo

Piazza dell'Arcivescovado 8, 56126 Pisa (PI)

The Museo dell'Opera del Duomo in English means the Museum of the Cathedral Works and this museum houses many of the works of art that were formerly kept in the city's cathedral or Duomo. The museum is located where the Episcopal seminary used to be in the square of Miracles.

The Museum was created to display all the medieval art which was previously scattered all over the structures in the square. The museum has about 200 paintings that

PISA TRAVEL GUIDE

date from the 12th to the 16th century. Among its exhibits are the sculptures that were created by the famous Italian sculptors Nicola Pisano and Giovanni Pisano. One of the highlights of a visit to this museum would be the ivory carving by Giovanni Pisano of the Madonna and child which he made for the altar. There are also marble decorations that look distinctly Moorish in design.

After the war other works of art were placed in the museum and it is now home to a collection of religious garments, manuscripts and other items from the cathedral, including models of the Duomo, which make up what is called the Cathedral collection. There are also some relics from Italy, and Egypt as well as some Etruscan relics that had been on display in other buildings

PISA TRAVEL GUIDE

in the Square of Miracles since the beginning of the 19th century.

One of the highlights of the display is a wooden crucifix form the 12th century and a bronze griffin that was brought back from the Crusades. Be sure to see the sketches of the frescoes of the Camposanto that were made during the restoration in the 19th century. The restorer created etchings and his son colored them in. The Museum has the prints of these etchings that show what the paintings in the Camposanto before the bombing during the war looked like.

The art is divided into rooms with the pieces related to the architecture of the Cathedral such as models and plans, being displayed in the first room. The Romanesque art such as the 12th century crucifix and the bronze griffin are in room 3, while room six houses the statues by Giovanno Pisano and other precious items such as a cross that was used to lead soldiers to battle during the first Crusade.

Perhaps one of the best the best reasons to visit the Museum other than the ancient artifacts is the great view that you get of the leaning tower next door from the second floor courtyard. The price of admission for the Museum is 5 Euros. The Museum is open from 9 am to 7:30 pm Monday to Saturday and on Sundays from 9 am to 1:45 pm.

🌐 Museo Nazionale di San Matteo

Piazza San Matteo in Soarta,

Lungarno Mediceo, 56100 Pisa

PISA TRAVEL GUIDE

Translated into English the name of this museum is the National Museum of St. Matthew. This museum is in a building on the waterfront north of the river Arno in central Pisa. The structure dates back to the 11th century. It was once a Benedictine convent and the original paintings are still visible on the walls. The museum collects religious works and has about 200 paintings. Some of the paintings and decorations on the walls are from the middle Ages and they have a distinctively Islamic feel.

Displayed in the museum are paintings and sculptures from the 12th to the 15 century from some of Italy's most famous artists including Madonna of Humility by Fra Angelico and St Paul by Masaccio. The museum also has as part of its collection Pisan sculptures from churches in

PISA TRAVEL GUIDE

the area that have been moved to the museum to protect them from pollution including several painted crosses. One noteworthy sculpture is a statue of the Madonna from the 14th century that was created by Andrea Pisano who is from the area. Copies of the sculptures have been put into the churches to replace the originals.

This museum is one of the most important in Europe for medieval art. It also has an important collection of art from Tuscany. The art is divided into sections with the sculptures and the older paintings being in the first room. There is also a section for manuscripts which are all lit including a bible with illustrations from the 11th century. It is definitely a place worth visiting and for 5.00 Euros you will certainly get your money's worth.

PISA TRAVEL GUIDE

The museum opens from 8:30 am to 7:00 pm most days except for Saturday and Sunday when it closes earlier at 1:00 pm and Mondays when it is closed.

🌐 Palazzo dell' Orologio

Piazza dei Cavalieri

56126 Pisa (PI), Italy

The name means Clock Palace or Tower and you can find it in the Piazza del Cavalieri.

Inside the building is the Library of the ScuolaNormaleSupiore but in the middle ages the Palazzo had a very different purpose.

PISA TRAVEL GUIDE

The Clock Tower was designed by Vasari and is made up of two buildings that were connected by a vault in the early 1600s. It used to be a place where old or sick Knights of the St. Stefano knighthood were sent. The two buildings were called the Torre deiGualandi and the Mansion del Capitano. When they were joined they were then named the Palazzo del Buon Uomo or Palace of the Good Man. In 1696 the clock which was formerly housed in the steeple of the church of St. Stefano was moved there and put in the arc that joins the two buildings. As a result the building was renamed to its current title. The small bell tower was put on the top of the building in 1696.

The building on the left is called the Palazzo della Giustizia, which was a tower house and in which could be found the offices of the city's magistrates. On the other

PISA TRAVEL GUIDE

side was the tower itself which was called dei Gualandi or Torre del Muda. The latter name refers to the eagle which is the symbol of the city. The tower has a tragic story and is sometimes called Torre della Fame or Hunger Tower because a nobleman, Count Ugolino della Gherardesca along with his family was killed by starvation while imprisoned there for treason. Legend has it that the count became so hungry that he ate the body of his dead grandchild. The poet Dante used this story in his epic the Divine Comedy.

The side of the Palace is decorated with frescoes by the like of Giovanni Stefano Maruscelli, and Lorenzo Paladini among others.

PISA TRAVEL GUIDE

🌐 Campanile di San Nicola (St. Nicolas Belfry)

Via Santa Maria

56100, Pisa, Italy

This is the second most famous bell tower in Pisa and it is located in the historical center of the city. St Nicolas Belfry was intended for the church which is next door. Its design is in the Pisan-Romanesque style and it was built in 1170 by Diotisalvi. The Belfry has eight sides and is made of limestone and Elba granite with Apuan marble for the columns. The bell tower is a hexagon in shape with a window on each side. There is only one bell in the tower. There is a staircase in the bell tower that is winding and that has a wall on the outer side only. It is said that this staircase was the inspiration for the one Renaissance architect Bramante put in the Vatican.

The tower is not open to the public but there is plenty to see from the outside.

🌐 Museum of the Ancient Ships

Medici Arsenale,

Ponte della Cittadella,

Pisa, Italy

These ships were found in 1998 when workers from the National Railway Company were digging in preparation for building an electrical station near the Pisa- San Rossore train station.

PISA TRAVEL GUIDE

They found the remains of a harbor and what later turned out to be 16 wooden ships which were later found to date back to between 200 BC and 500 AD. Some of them were very well preserved and investigations have led them to believe that the ships are Roman. They are the only ships of this kind to be found in such good condition. Some of the ships still had cargo on them. Some of the items found were tall Roman jars, called amphorae containing preserved fruit such as plums and cherries as well as olives. One boat had a leather sandal and a wicker basket. Archeologists who were brought to the site also found stone, iron and wooden anchors as well as ropes and fishing equipment. The finds tell a lot about life in ancient Etruscan and Roman times as well as life in ancient Pisa.

PISA TRAVEL GUIDE

Although the official Museum of the Ancient Ships is still being constructed there is an exhibition that is open to the public every day of the week. On weekends you can visit without reservations if you go between 10am and 12 noon or between 2:30 and 3:30 pm. During the week reservations must be made. It contains examples of all the artifacts found including the personal items of the sailors. A tour of the museum will also teach you about the floods that led to the submersion of the harbor and the ships.

🌐 Ussero Café

Lungarno Pacinotti 27

Palazzo dell' Ussero

56126 Pisa

PISA TRAVEL GUIDE

The Caffedell'Ussero is a coffee house in a red brick structure called the Palazzo Agostini which is located on the right side of the river Arno. The cafe is in a Gothic building that was constructed in the 15th century. Café dell'Ussero was opened in 1775 and gets its name from the Italian word ussaro which refers to a soldier in the cavalry. It is one of the oldest cafes in Europe. The word is originally Hungarian and came to Italy via France.

The cafe once had a reputation for being the meeting place of Pisa's scholars from the nearby university. It was also a favorite of the followers of the pro- politician Mazzini and some of the more liberal university lecturers. They gathered in the café to drink coffee, play billiards and discuss their political views. There is confirmation of

PISA TRAVEL GUIDE

these meetings in the town's police records from that time.

The café was turned into a cinema at the end of the 19th century. It was one of the first cinemas in the region. When the First World War ended Ussero was once again turned into a coffee house and the artists and literary types returned. Even today it is still a favorite haunt of the city's artists.

There are many stories of significant events that took place in this café and the walls carry testimony to many important and visitors. There are letters and other documents displayed that confirm the age and history of the establishment.

PISA TRAVEL GUIDE

One of them the legends associated with the cafe is that in 1839 the Ussero café played host to meetings of the First Italian Congress of Scientists. The café has also seen other famous visitors such as the first director of the newspaper La Nazione, Alessandro D'Ancona and the Italian poet GuiseppiGiusti who talked of visiting the café in his memoirs. Other famous people who spent time at the Café include Charles Lindberg and the founder of the Futurist movement Gulieelmo Marconi. Many students from the local university spent time at the café and some of them have gone on to become Prime Ministers and Presidents and even receive the Noble Prize. There was even a collection of essays written about the coffee house called " L'Ussero: Un Caffe 'Universidario' nella Vita di Pisa". The café is open Monday to Friday 9am to 7pm.

PISA TRAVEL GUIDE

Budget Tips

🌐 Accommodation

Hotel Granduca Tuscany

Via San GiulianoTerme 13, 56017

Pisa, Tuscany, Italy

Telephone: (+39) 050815029

www.hotelgranduca.it

PISA TRAVEL GUIDE

This is a fairly new hotel which has parking, Internet access and a restaurant where a buffet breakfast is included at no extra charge.

The Hotel Granduca is next to a sporting center and guests are allowed to use the heated swimming pool and tennis courts. The hotel also has its own Wellness Center.

Hotel Granducca has 170 soundproof rooms and every guest has a television, a radio and a telephone. Some rooms have terraces. The hotel is conveniently located near to the main train station and it is also close to the thermal spa of San Giuliano. The price of a double room is $57 US per night.

PISA TRAVEL GUIDE

Hotel Capitol

Via Enrico Fermi 13, 56126

Pisa, Tuscany, Italy

Telephone: (+39) 5049557

http://www.hotelcapitol.pisa.it

This hotel is located in the center of the city close to the University of Pisa in a historic old building but with very modern furnishing. It is ideally located in walking distance of the main visitor sights and is also close to shops and restaurants so you can leave your car in the parking lot and walk to wherever you want to go. For the animal lovers pets are allowed at this hotel.

PISA TRAVEL GUIDE

Hotel Capitol has an internal courtyard as well as a lounge area and bar. The price of a double room is $97 US per night.

Hotel la Torre

Via Cesare Battisti 17, 56126,

Pisa, Tuscany, Italy

Telephone: (+39) 05025220

Hotel la Torre is in the city center near to the sights that are on every visitor's list including the Piazza deiMiracoli and the Pisa Royal Palace. It offers free wireless internet, and satellite TV. and phones in every room as well as multi-lingual staff and a free buffet breakfast.

PISA TRAVEL GUIDE

A single room with a private bathroom is $80 US per night and a double is $94.

Hotel Francesco

Via Santa Maria, 129, 56126, Pisa, Italy

Telephone: (+39) 050 555453

http://www.hotlefrancesco.com

Hotel Francesco can be found in the center of Pisa in a very old building that has been renovated to house the hotel. It is close to all the famous historical sites and to the airport. In fact it is on the same street that leads to the Leaning Tower.

PISA TRAVEL GUIDE

The hotel offers free internet and phone calls, a large terrace, and a restaurant that specializes in Tuscan dishes. The price of a double room is $128 US

Eden Park Tuscany Resort

Via Enrico Fermi 11, 56126,

Pisa, Tuscany, Italy

Telephone #: (+39) 050870252

http://www.edenparkpisa.it

Nestled in the Tuscan countryside near to the river, this resort is still close to the City center and the main sights. It is consists of 30 apartments each with 2 rooms which are in cottages and is surrounded by forest. There are several medieval villages nearby and a great view of the hills. Each cottage has its own kitchen and private access.

PISA TRAVEL GUIDE

The resort offers nature tours, horseback riding, and paragliding. It is the perfect location for couples or families that want to get away from it all. The price of a single is $82 US while a double is $ 41 per person and a triple $36. Breakfast costs $10

🌐 Restaurants, Cafés & Bars

Il Montino

Vicolo del Moule 1,

Pisa, Italy

Il Montino is a pizzeria that offers the option of dining in or having take out.

PISA TRAVEL GUIDE

There are only a few tables so get there early if you intend to eat in. the cost of a slice of pizza is Euro 1.50 while the average price of a meal is between $21 and $29. The pizzeria is open from 10:30 am to 3:00 pm then 5:00 pm to 10:00 pm Monday to Saturday.

Ristorante Turrido

Via D. Cavalca 64, Santa Maria,

Pisa, Italy

This indoor/outdoor restaurant is 20 minutes from the Leaning Tower and is known for its Tuscan dishes especially its pesto. The locals eat there and there is usually no better recommendation. This restaurant is also known to offer a wide array of desserts. It's open Monday to Saturday 6:30 pm to 10:30 pm

PISA TRAVEL GUIDE

Peperosa Pisa

Via Renato Fucini N 10, 56126

Pisa, Italy

Telephone: (+39) 0503144170

The eatery offers Italian and Mediterranean fare and also has a wine bar. It is recommended that you make reservations. Prices for a meal range between $13 and $39 US and Peperisa is open Sunday through Saturday 11:00 am to 3:30 pm and 7:00 am to 12:00 midnight.

L'Ostellino

Piazza Felice Cavallotti 1

56126 Pisa

This diner is known for its sandwiches as it has a very

wide assortment of fillings and fresh vegetables. Most of the sandwiches are available for between $4 and $8 and there are also meals available. L'Ostellino also has a bar so everything you need is in one place. The dress code for this diner is casual and no reservations are necessary. The restaurant does take out but not delivery and be sure to walk with cash or a debit card because credit cards are not accepted.

Coccio Bar & Gelateria

Via Santa Maria 86,

Pisa, Italy

This little restaurant specializes in local Italian cuisine and ice cream. It's near the leaning Tower and is known to offer a delicious breakfast. This eatery is known for its cappuccino as well as its salad. Coccio also serves sandwiches and other typical café food. Most of the fare at Coccio Bar can be had for under $10 US and the staff has a reputation for being very courteous and quick.

Shopping

Corso Italia

The Corso Italia is the High Street of Pisa with many shops and a lot to offer the shopper who does not want to spend a deal of money. It is usually a very busy and crowded street in the quarter of San Marino. On this street is a commercial center called the Corte di San Domenico. Further down the street near to the river a monthly antique market is held in a 17th century building called the Logge dei Banchi which used to be a jail.

PISA TRAVEL GUIDE

The Corso Italia is also a good place to get a trendy haircut or buy a comic book for a specialty shop known as Fumettando. After working up an appetite from all the walking you can grab a slice of Pisan pizza or even buy a Nutella wafer.

Borgo Stretto

This street offers high-end shopping and boasts expensive shops and boutiques. Take a walk under the archways and watch the lovely window displays. When you need a break from shopping there are many cafes and ice cream parlors. Examples of shops to be found on this street are Valenti which has been in business since the 70s and which carries the latest in designer fashions for men and women and BB Maison. There are also stringed instrument shops that are a must for any visiting musician.

If you happen to be in Pisa at Christmas there is a market on Borgo Stretto where you can get some of the designer duds for less. There are also markets and shops on the side streets off of Borgo Stretto that offer better bargains.

Piazza dei Cavalieri & Ponti di Mezzo

There are open markets on these streets on the 2nd weekend of every month. These markets are a good place to find antiques at an affordable price. If you find something that appears to be too good a deal then it probably is so be very careful about what you purchase. It

PISA TRAVEL GUIDE

should be noted that the markets do not open in the months of July and August.

Piazza delle Vettovaglie

Scaliaureliosaffi

Livorno, 57123

This square is over one hundred years old and houses many shops as well as a fruit and food market. This is a good place to purchase wines and grocery items. It is also called the Central Market and is the largest indoor market in Europe. It is a covered market and is always very busy with people looking for fresh fruit and vegetables. Do not miss an opportunity to try the bread on sale especially the Tuscan 'saltless' bread or the star of the market the

PISA TRAVEL GUIDE

labronica or Pavilion fish which has been extremely popular for many years.

There are over 200 shops in the market as well as scores of wineries in the basement which can be accessed from two side doors and down the stairs. The market is also a wholesale market. There are also bars and cafes and it is open Monday to Friday from 7:00 am until 1:30 pm.

Via Buonarroti & Via San Martino

If you are looking for thrift shops and bargain shops then these two streets are the place to go. Via Buonarrotiis a busy market and both street markets open every Wednesday and Saturday. You can find clothes at these markets as well as fashion accessories and other items.

PISA TRAVEL GUIDE

Via Buonarroti offers many souvenirs and is one of the places where the locals shop.

PISA TRAVEL GUIDE

Know Before You Go

🌍 Entry Requirements

By virtue of the Schengen agreement, travellers from other countries in the European Union do not need a visa when visiting Italy. Additionally Swiss travellers are also exempt. Visitors from certain other countries such as the USA, Canada, Japan, Israel, Australia and New Zealand do not need visas if their stay in Italy does not exceed 90 days. When entering Italy you will be required to make a declaration of presence, either at the airport, or at a police station within eight days of arrival. This applies to visitors from other Schengen countries, as well as those visiting from non-Schengen countries.

🌍 Health Insurance

Citizens of other EU countries are covered for emergency health care in Italy. UK residents, as well as visitors from Switzerland are covered by the European Health Insurance Card (EHIC), which can be applied for free of charge. Visitors from non-Schengen countries will need to show proof of private health insurance that is valid for the duration of their stay in Italy (that offers at least €37,500 coverage), as part of their visa application. No special vaccinations are required.

PISA TRAVEL GUIDE

🌐 Travelling with Pets

Italy participates in the Pet Travel Scheme (PETS) which allows UK residents to travel with their pets without requiring quarantine upon re-entry. Certain conditions will need to be met. The animal will have to be microchipped and up to date on rabies vaccinations. In the case of dogs, a vaccination against canine distemper is also required by the Italian authorities. When travelling from the USA, your pet will need to be microchipped or marked with an identifying tattoo and up to date on rabies vaccinations. An EU Annex IV Veterinary Certificate for Italy will need to be issued by an accredited veterinarian. On arrival in Italy, you can apply for an EU pet passport to ease your travel in other EU countries.

🌐 Airports

Fiumicino – Leonardo da Vinci International Airport (FCO) is one of the busiest airports in Europe and the main international airport of Italy. It is located about 35km southwest of the historical quarter of Rome. Terminal 5 is used for trans-Atlantic and international flights, while Terminals 1, 2 and 3 serve mainly for domestic flights and medium haul flights to other European destinations. Before Leonardo da Vinci replaced it, the **Ciampino–G. B. Pastine International Airport** (CIA)

PISA TRAVEL GUIDE

was the main international airport servicing Rome and Italy. It is one of the oldest airports in the country still in use. Although it declined in importance, budget airlines such as Ryanair boosted its air traffic in recent years. The airport is used by Wizz Air, V Bird, Helvetic, Transavia Airlines, Sterling, Ryanair, Thomsonfly, EasyJet, Air Berlin, Hapag-Lloyd Express and Carpatair.

Milan Malpensa Airport (MXP) is the largest of the three airports serving the city of Milan. Located about 40km northwest of Milan's city center, it connects travellers to the regions of Lombardy, Piedmont and Liguria. **Milan Linate Airport** (LIN) is Milan's second international airport. **Venice Marco Polo Airport** (VCE) provides access to the charms of Venice. **Olbia Costa Smeralda Airport** (OLB) is located near Olbia, Sardinia. Main regional airports are **Guglielmo Marconi Airport** (BLQ), an international airport servicing the region of Bologna, **Capodichino Airport** at Naples (NAP), **Pisa International Airport** (PSA), formerly Galileo Galilei Airport, the main airport serving Tuscany, **Sandro Pertini Airport** near Turin (TRN), **Cristoforo Colombo** in Genoa (GOA), **Punta Raisi Airport** in Palermo (PMO), **Vincenzo Bellini Airport** in Catania (CTA) and **Palese Airport** in Bari (BRI).

Airlines

Alitalia is the flag carrier and national airline of Italy. It has a subsidiary, Alitalia CityLiner, which operates short-haul regional flights. Air Dolomiti is a regional Italian based subsidiary of of the Lufthansa Group. Meridiana is a privately owned airline based at Olbia in Sardinia.

Fiumicino - Leonardo da Vinci International Airport serves as the main hub for Alitalia, which has secondary hubs at Milan Linate and Milan Malpensa Airport. Alitalia CityLiner uses Fiumicino – Leonardo da Vinci International Airport as main hub and has secondary hubs at Milan-Linate, Naples and Trieste. Fiumicino – Leonardo da Vinci International Airport is also one of two primary hubs used by the budget Spanish airline Vueling. Milan Malpensa Airport is one of the largest bases for the British budget airline EasyJet. Venice Airport serves as an Italian base for the Spanish budget airline, Volotea, which provides connections mainly to other destinations in Europe. Olbia Costa Smeralda Airport (OLB), located near Olbia, Sardinia is the primary base of Meridiana, a private Italian Airline in partnership with Air Italia and Fly Egypt.

PISA TRAVEL GUIDE

🌐 Currency

Italy's currency is the Euro. It is issued in notes in denominations of €500, €200, €100, €50, €20, €10 and €5. Coins are issued in denominations of €2, €1, 50c, 20c, 10c, 5c, 2c and 1c.

🌐 Banking & ATMs

Using ATMs or Bancomats, as they are known in Italy, to withdraw money is simple if your ATM card is compatible with the MasterCard/Cirrus or Visa/Plus networks. There is a €250 limit on daily withdrawals. Italian machines are configured for 4-digit PIN numbers, although some machines will be able to handle longer PIN numbers. Bear in mind some Bancomats can run out of cash over weekends and that the more remote villages may not have adequate banking facilities so plan ahead.

🌐 Credit Cards

Credit cards are valid tender in most Italian businesses. While Visa and MasterCard are accepted universally, most tourist oriented businesses also accept American Express and Diners Club. Credit cards issued in Europe are smart cards that that are fitted with a microchip and require a PIN for each transaction.

PISA TRAVEL GUIDE

This means that a few ticket machines, self-service vendors and other businesses may not be configured to accept the older magnetic strip credit cards. Do remember to advise your bank or credit card company of your travel plans before leaving.

🌐 Tourist Taxes

Tourist tax varies from city to city, as each municipality sets its own rate. The money is collected by your accommodation and depends on the standard of accommodation. A five star establishment will levy a higher amount than a four star or three star establishment. You can expect to pay somewhere between €1 and €7 per night, with popular destinations like Rome, Venice, Milan and Florence charging a higher overall rate. In some regions, the rate is also adjusted seasonally. Children are usually exempt until at least the age of 10 and sometimes up to the age of 18. In certain areas, disabled persons and their companions also qualify for discounted rates. Tourist tax is payable directly to the hotel or guesthouse before the end of your stay.

🌐 Reclaiming VAT

If you are not from the European Union, you can claim back VAT (Value Added Tax) paid on your purchases in Italy. The

PISA TRAVEL GUIDE

VAT rate in Italy is 21 percent and this can be claimed back on your purchases if certain conditions are met. The merchant needs to be partnered with a VAT refund program. This will be indicated if the shop displays a "Tax Free" sign. The shop assistant will fill out a form for reclaiming VAT. When you submit this at the airport, you will receive your refund.

🌏 Tipping Policy

If your bill includes the phrase "coperto e servizio", that means that a service charge or tip is already included. Most waiting staff in Italy are salaried workers, but if the service is excellent, a few euros extra would be appreciated.

🌏 Mobile Phones

Most EU countries, including Italy use the GSM mobile service. This means that most UK phones and some US and Canadian phones and mobile devices will work in Italy. While you could check with your service provider about coverage before you leave, using your own service in roaming mode will involve additional costs. The alternative is to purchase an Italian SIM card to use during your stay in Italy.
Italy has four mobile networks. They are TIM, Wind, Vodafone and Tre (3) and they all provide pre-paid services. TIM offers

PISA TRAVEL GUIDE

two tourist options, both priced at €20 (+ €10 for the SIM card) with a choice of two packages - 2Gb data, plus 200 minutes call time or internet access only with a data allowance of 5Gb. Vodafone, Italy's second largest network offers a Vodafone Holiday package including SIM card for €30. They also offer the cheapest roaming rates. Wind offers an Italian Tourist pass for €20 which includes 100 minutes call time and 2Gb data and can be extended with a restart option for an extra €10.

To purchase a local SIM card, you will need to show your passport or some other form of identification and provide your residential details in Italy. By law, SIM registration is required prior to activation. Most Italian SIM cards expire after a 90 day period of inactivity. When dialling internationally, remember to use the (+) sign and the code of the country you are connecting to.

🌐 Dialling Code

The international dialling code for Italy is +39.

🌐 Emergency Numbers

Police: 113

Fire: 115

Ambulance: 118

PISA TRAVEL GUIDE

MasterCard: 800 789 525

Visa: 800 819 014

🌐 Public Holidays

1 January: New Year's Day (Capodanno)

6 January: Day of the Epiphany (Epifania)

March-April: Easter Monday (Lunedì dell'Angelo or Pasquetta)

25 April: Liberation Day (Festa della Liberazione)

1 May: International Worker's Day (Festa del Lavoro / Festa dei Lavoratori)

2 June: Republic Day (Festa della Repubblica)

15 August: Assumption Day (Ferragosto / Assunta)

1 November: All Saints Day (Tutti i santi / Ognissanti)

8 December: Immaculate Conception (Immacolata Concezione / Immacolata)

25 December: Christmas Day (Natale)

26 December: St Stephen's Day (Santo Stefano)

A number of Saints days are observed regionally throughout the year.

🌐 Time Zone

Italy falls in the Central European Time Zone. This can be calculated as Greenwich Mean Time/Coordinated Universal

PISA TRAVEL GUIDE

Time (GMT/UTC) +2; Eastern Standard Time (North America) -6; Pacific Standard Time (North America) -9.

🌐 Daylight Savings Time

Clocks are set forward one hour on 29 March and set back one hour on 25 October for Daylight Savings Time.

🌐 School Holidays

The academic year begins in mid September and ends in mid June. The summer holiday is from mid June to mid September, although the exact times may vary according to region. There are short breaks around Christmas and New Year and also during Easter. Some regions such as Venice and Trentino have an additional break during February for the carnival season.

🌐 Trading Hours

Trading hours for the majority of shops are from 9am to 12.30pm and then again from 3.30pm to 7.30pm, although in some areas, the second shift may be from 4pm to 8pm instead. The period between 1pm and 4pm is known in Italy as the *riposo*. Large department shops and malls tend to be open from 9am to 9pm, from Monday to Saturday. Post offices are open

PISA TRAVEL GUIDE

from 8.30am to 1.30pm from Monday to Saturday. Most shops and many restaurants are closed on Sundays. Banking hours are from 8.30am to 1.30pm and then again from 3pm to 4pm, Monday to Friday. Most restaurants are open from noon till 2.30pm and then again from 7pm till 11pm or midnight, depending on the establishment. Nightclubs open around 10pm, but only liven up after midnight. Closing times vary, but will generally be between 2am and 4am. Museum hours vary, although major sights tend to be open continuously and often up to 7.30pm. Many museums are closed on Mondays.

🌐 Driving Laws

The Italians drive on the right hand side of the road. A driver's licence from any of the European Union member countries is valid in Italy. Visitors from non-EU countries will require an International Driving Permit that must remain current throughout the duration of their stay in Italy.

The speed limit on Italy's autostrade is 130km per hour and 110km per hour on main extra-urban roads, but this is reduced by 20km to 110km and 90km respectively in rainy weather. On secondary extra-urban roads, the speed limit is 90km per hour; on urban highways, it is 70km per hour and on urban roads, the speed limit is 50km per hour. You are not allowed to drive in the ZTL or Limited Traffic Zone (or *zona traffico limitato* in Italian) unless you have a special permit.

Visitors to Italy are allowed to drive their own non-Italian vehicles in the country for a period of up to six months. After this, they will be required to obtain Italian registration with Italian licence plates. Italy has very strict laws against driving under the influence of alcohol. The blood alcohol limit is 0.05 and drivers caught above the limit face penalties such as fines of up to €6000, confiscation of their vehicles, suspension of their licenses and imprisonment of up to 6 months. Breathalyzer tests are routine at accident scenes.

🌐 Drinking Laws

The legal drinking age in Italy is 16. While drinking in public spaces is allowed, public drunkenness is not tolerated. Alcohol is sold in bars, wine shops, liquor stores and grocery shops.

🌐 Smoking Laws

In 2005, Italy implemented a policy banning smoking from public places such as bars, restaurants, nightclubs and working places, limiting it to specially designated smoking rooms. Further legislation banning smoking from parks, beaches and stadiums is being explored.

PISA TRAVEL GUIDE

🌐 Electricity

Electricity: 220 volts

Frequency: 50 Hz

Italian electricity sockets are compatible with the Type L plugs, a plug that features three round pins or prongs, arranged in a straight line. An alternate is the two-pronged Type C Euro adaptor. If travelling from the USA, you will need a power converter or transformer to convert the voltage from 220 to 110, to avoid damage to your appliances. The latest models of many laptops, camcorders, mobile phones and digital cameras are dual-voltage with a built in converter.

🌐 Tourist Information (TI)

There are tourist information (TI) desks at each of the terminals of the Leonardo da Vinci International Airport, as well as interactive Information kiosks with the latest touch-screen technology. In Rome, the tourist office can be found at 5 Via Parigi, near the Termini Station and it is identified as APT, which stands for Azienda provinciale del Turismo. Free maps and brochures of current events are available from tourist kiosks.

Several of the more tourist-oriented regions of Italy offer tourist cards that include admission to most of the city's attractions.

PISA TRAVEL GUIDE

While these cards are not free, some offer great value for money. A variety of tourism apps are also available online.

🌐 Food & Drink

Pasta is a central element of many typically Italian dishes, but there are regional varieties and different types of pasta are matched to different sauces. Well known pasta dishes such as lasagne and bolognaise originated in Bologna. Stuffed pasta is popular in the northern part of Italy, while the abundance of seafood and olives influences southern Italian cuisine. As far as pizza goes, the Italians differentiate between the thicker Neapolitan pizza and the thin crust Roman pizza, as well as white pizza, also known as focaccia and tomato based pizza. Other standards include minestrone soup, risotto, polenta and a variety of cheeses, hams, sausages and salamis. If you are on a budget, consider snacking on stuzzichini with a few drinks during happy hour which is often between 7 and 9pm. The fare can include salami, cheeses, cured meat, mini pizzas, bread, vegetables, pastries or pate. In Italy, Parmesan refers only to cheese originating from the area surrounding Parma. Favorites desserts include tiramisu or Italian gelato.

Italians enjoy relaxing to aperitifs before they settle down to a meal and their favorites are Campari, Aperol or Negroni, the famous Italian cocktail. Wine is enjoyed with dinner. Italy is particularly famous for its red wines. The best known wine regions are Piedmont, which produces robust and dry reds, Tuscany and Alto Adige, where Alpine soil adds a distinctive acidity. After the meal, they settle down to a glass of limoncello, the country's most popular liqueur, or grappa, which is distilled from grape seeds and stems, as digestive. Other options in this class include a nut liqueur, nocino, strawberry based Fragolino Veneto or herbal digestives like gineprino, laurino or mirto. Italians are also fond of coffee. Espresso is drunk through throughout the day, but cappuccino is considered a morning drink. The most popular beers in Italy are Peroni and Moretti.

Websites

http://vistoperitalia.esteri.it/home/en
This is the website of the Consulate General of Italy. Here you can look up whether you will need a visa and also process your application online.
http://www.italia.it/en/home.html
The official website of Italian tourism
http://www.italia.it/en/useful-info/mobile-apps.html
Select the region of your choice to download a useful mobile app to your phone.
http://www.italylogue.com/tourism

PISA TRAVEL GUIDE

http://italiantourism.com/index.html

http://www.reidsitaly.com/

http://wikitravel.org/en/Italy

https://www.summerinitaly.com/

http://www.accessibleitalianholiday.com/

Planning Italian vacations around the needs of disabled tourists.

CPSIA information can be obtained
at www.ICGtesting.com
Printed in the USA
LVOW10s2018050217
523261LV00016B/835/P

9 781533 052124